4.9.2001

 Bayerisc
Schlösse
Bavarian /
of State C

C000001664

Herrenchiemsee

by Elmar D. Schmid

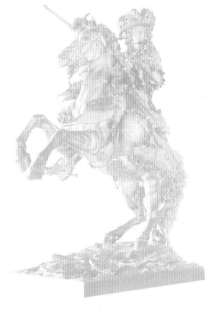

Prestel
Munich · London · New York

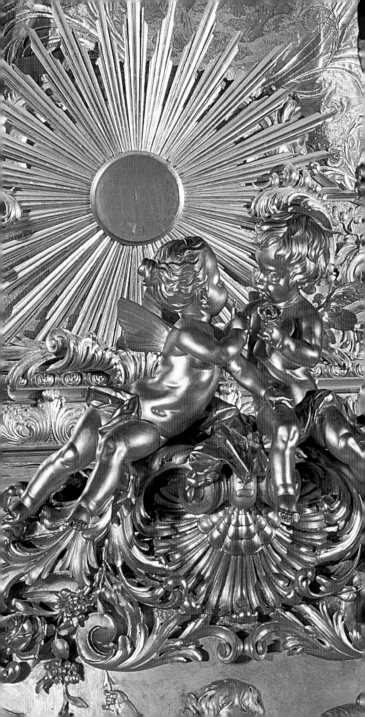

CONTENTS

following double page: The Chiemsee royal palace, modelled on Versailles,
was intended "to be a sort of temple to fame in which I can honour the
memory of King Louis XIV" (King Ludwig II)

left: The sun symbol in the bedchamber (Room 13)

3

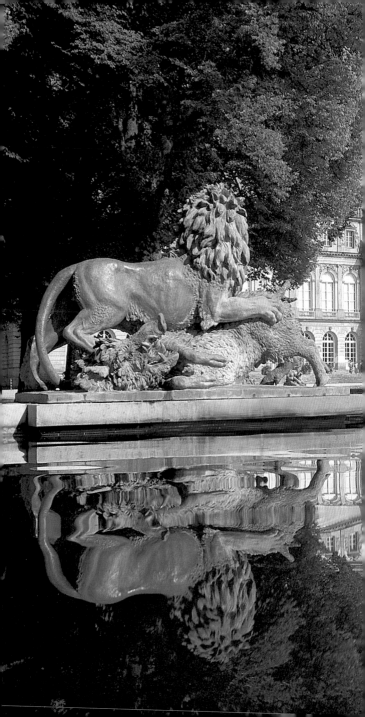

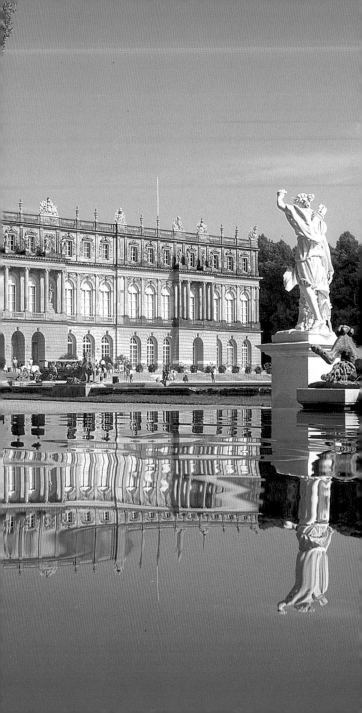

INTRODUCTION

Neuschwanstein, Linderhof and Herrenchiemsee—King Ludwig II of Bavaria's palatial residences—make such an impact not only because the buildings and their grounds are splendid, but also because their superb landscape settings in the Bavarian Alps more than match their grandeur. Neuschwanstein is a fairy-tale mountain fortress resplendent against the bizarre panorama of the Tannheim mountains; Linderhof is a dreamy haven, hidden away in a sunny valley of the Ammer Range and Herrenchiemsee is a grand palace on an island in the sweeping landscape of the Chiemgau. "The spot is one of the most beautiful to be found anywhere, sacred and inaccessible ... ," wrote Ludwig II to Richard Wagner on 13 May 1868 refering to his Neuschwanstein project, emphasizing the magnificent views the site afforded of the Säuling, the Tyrolean mountains and out across the Schwangau plain.

All the king's castles and palaces are 'sacred and inaccessible'. The awe-inspiring landscapes in which they are set are what make them so compelling.

View from the Augustinian Canon towards the shoreline of Herreninsel with the Chiemgau mountains in the background

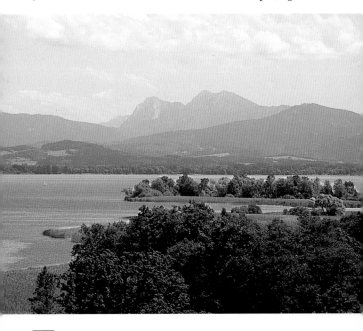

From Island Monastery to Augustinian Canon and Cathedral Chapter

Herreninsel, the largest island in Lake Chiemsee, was first settled long ago. Archaeological finds go back as far as the Bronze Age Urnfield culture (1200–750 BC). An early medieval rampart at the south-west tip of the island was a refuge in times of danger.

The Benedictine Abbey on Herreninsel must have been one of the earliest such foundations in Bavaria. Recent excavation has uncovered traces of wooden buildings dating from the first half of the 7th century on the site of the present monastery square on the north tip of the island. Renovated once, they were later replaced by stone buildings in the mid-8th century. These buildings may represent the nucleus of St Salvator Abbey, which stood on the same site.

In the mid-8th century a church with a single nave and a separate room to the east stood on the site of the present 'island cathedral'. The church, the convent building and the cloister were remodelled in about

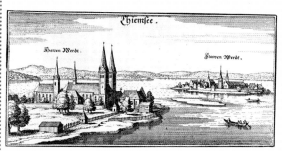

The island's ecclesiastic foundations of Herren- and Frauen-chiemsee, *Topographia Bavariae* by Matthias Merian, 1644

800 to form a close. Fragments of a chancel screen, some of which were found among the rubble, came from the monastery church dating from the Caroligian period. In 788 Charlemagne transferred the monastery to the Archbishop of Metz; in the 9th century it passed to the Archbishop of Salzburg.

Conrad I founded the Herrenchiemsee chapter of Augustinian canons around 1125/30 which resulted in the decaying religious establishment flourishing again. Its renown continued to grow after Archbishop

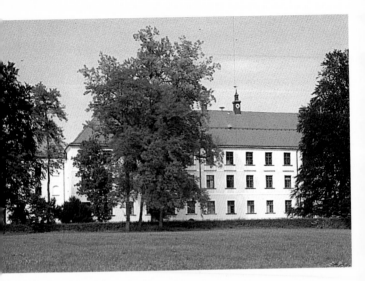

Herren-
chiemsee
Monastery,
the Princes'
floor wing
from the
south-west

Eberhard II of Salzburg founded the Chiemsee diocese in 1217, thus elevating the Herreninsel collegiate church to cathedral status.

The Baroque cathedral chapter with its gardens, meadows and fields, is depicted as the 'Kingdom of God on Earth' surrounded by the waters of Lake Chiemsee, in a large fresco (c. 1770) in the prelate's office (accessible via the Exter Gallery, see p. 12). The Chiemgau religious foundation was long known as the 'Herrenchiemsee Cathedral Chapter and Monastery'.

Secularization in 1803 disbanded the Augustinian canons and the cathedral was ultimately deconsecrated in 1807. The Chiemsee Bishopric was abolished in 1808. The first secular proprietor of the island was Carl von Lüneschloss, a wealthy Mannheim merchant. Buildings were demolished, a brewery was housed in the cathedral and all the fittings were sold at auction. The island was to change hands many times.

'Conclude the sale immediately, the premises seem appropriate. Ludwig.' In this telegram sent on 4 September 1873 to Lorenz von Düfflipp, Counsellor to the Bavarian Court, King Ludwig II ordered him to buy the island so that the monarch could build a new

The Old Parish Church of St Mary

palace which would be a 'second Versailles'. The island was acquired by the king for 350,000 guilders (fl.) and promptly surveyed. Ludwig II had several rooms in the monastery tracts renovated and furnished for his own use. He first lived in what is now known as the 'Altes Schloss' from 30 April until 2 May 1875. The corner-stone was laid for the 'Königliches Schloss Herrenchiemsee' on 21 May 1878. It is

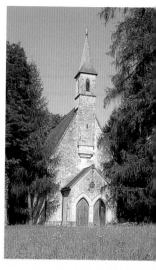

sometimes also called the 'Neues Schloss' (see p. 14).

The Augustinian Canons and Cathedral Chapter today

Steep steps lead up from the landing-stage to the former monastic buildings. Built to incorporate remains of a medieval structure, the present appearance of the

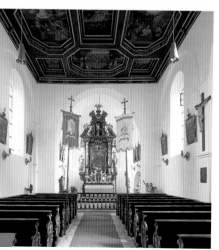

complex is Baroque. Partly demolished and put to profane use as a brewery (not open to the public) after 1807, the **Collegiate Church** (1676–79) stands in front of the square monastery complex. The **Convention floor** (east wing,

The Old Parish Church, view of the altar

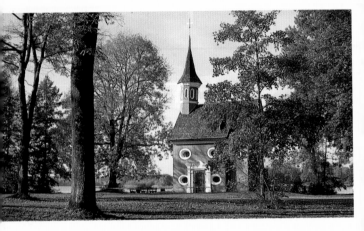

Baroque lakeside chapel on the northern shore

1645–49), the **Princes' floor** (south wing, 1700–16), the **Brewery floor** (west wing, 1661–65) and the **Prelate's Office floor** (north wing, 1727–30) enclose a lovely monastery courtyard laid out as a rose garden. Other parts of the Cathedral Chapter include the Late Gothic **Old Parish Church** with a Baroque interior, the **Seminary Building** (1737–40, now a restaurant and hotel), the outbuildings (renovated in the 19th century) and the **Lake Chapel** (1697), down below on the north shore of the lake.

The buildings of the former religious foundation dominate the northern tip of the island like a 'mighty fortress to God'. Restored to their light colour again, the façades are visible from far out on the lake. From the Baroque garden terrace, which was planted with plane trees in 1893, the view stretches east across Lake Chiemsee to the island called Fraueninsel, the seat of an early medieval nunnery. The nunnery and the fishing village on Herreninsel's twin island invite the eye to linger on a timeless, idyllic scene.

The Museum in the Augustinian Chapterhouse

Part of the Augustinian complex has been open to the public since 1998. The **Museum** on the **Convention floor** (east wing) has been convincingly incorporated in

Convention floor, formerly King Ludwig II's private apartments: the study

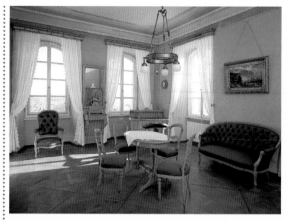

the Baroque architecture. 'From monastery to royal palace' deals with the development and importance of Herrenchiemsee as an ecclesiastical centre and, through its original exhibits, documents its turbulent and ultimately tragic history. Highlights are sections

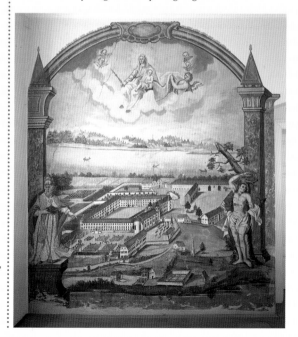

Prelate's Office floor, mural with a view of the island monastery, c. 1770

of the cloister and the magnificent library dating from 1737/39, a vaulted hall with two aisles, decorated with stucco and paintings by the brilliant Munich court artist Johann Baptist Zimmermann.

On the first floor are the rooms Ludwig II had renovated for his own use around 1875. His dining-room (on the **Princes' floor**, south wing) was occupied from 10 to 24 August 1948 by the Constitutional Convention which met here to discuss a constitution for the fledgling Federal Republic of Germany. Several rooms in this part of the Museum document the steps taken before drafting the Republic's 'Basic Law'.

Since 2001 parts of the Prelate's Office floor (north wing) have been added to the Museum. Seven Baroque rooms house a gallery with paintings by Julius Exter (1863–1939), who spent his last years in Übersee-Feldwies on Lake Chiemsee. He was a pioneering exponent of modern painting in fin-de-siècle Munich, a hotbed of avant-garde art movements in 1900 in the era of Luitpold, the Prince Regent. Rivalling the fame of his contemporary, the painter Franz von Stuck, Exter was

Prelate's Office floor, Julius Exter gallery, *Mountains*, Chiemgau landscape with the Alps *c*. 1925

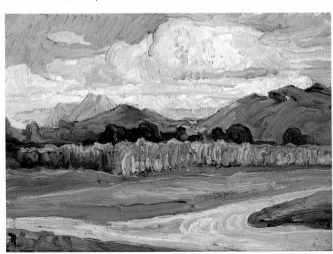

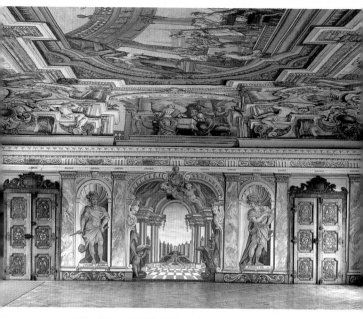

Princes' floor, the Kaisersaal with Baroque frescoes from 1713/15

acclaimed throughout Europe during his lifetime. Recalling Emil Nolde, the exuberant palette of Exter's late work is Expressionist in feeling and represents a high point of early Modern south German art. With all periods of the artist's work represented, the gallery supplements the exhibits in the **Exter-Haus** museum in Übersee-Feldwies.

Although most of it is not open to the public, the **Princes' floor** (south wing) had apartments for high-ranking visitors, including the Prince-Bishops of Chiemsee who resided in Salzburg. The former reception room, called the **Garden Room** or **Fürstenzimmer** (Prince's Chamber), is decorated with illusionist frescoes. The **Kaisersaal** (Emperor's Chamber) or **Fürstensaal**, is also frescoed throughout. Statues of the first twelve Roman emperors as well as New Testament scenes featuring the theme of banquets and foods supplement the High Baroque illusionist architecture. The magnificent frescoes, dating from 1713–15, are the work of the Munich painter Benedikt Albrecht.

The boundless admiration felt by Ludwig II of Bavaria for the ill-fated House of Bourbon in France found a special form of expression through the construction of the palatial residences at Linderhof and Herrenchiemsee. In his search for the idealism of monarchy, unhampered by any ties with reality, Ludwig II viewed French absolutism as the purest embodiment of royal power and majesty. He made a cult of idolizing Louis XIV, Louis XV and Louis XVI of France as mystically transfigured heroes. The name Ludwig is the German form of Louis; Louis XVI of France was godfather to Ludwig I of Bavaria, who in turn was Ludwig II's grandfather. The young king's enthusiasm for the French royal family dated from the first time he went to Paris and travelled through other areas of France in July 1867. Although Ludwig II had no time for Versailles on that first trip, by 1868 he had commissioned the court architect, Georg von Doll-mann, to design a palace modelled on the chief rooms in Versailles, including the royal bedchamber and the Hall of Mirrors with the two adjacent halls. It was at

The palace, garden front with Latona, Fama and Fortuna fountains

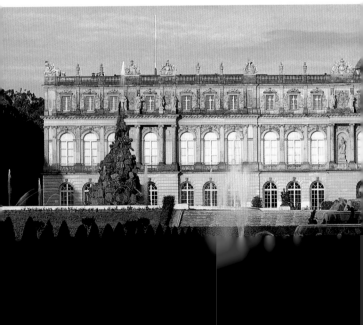

first planned to build the palace at Linderhof in the Graswang Valley.

The Versailles projects, which resulted in thirteen different plans being drafted altogether, became increasingly elaborate from 1870 onwards, ultimately approaching the scale and appearance of the original. King Ludwig II immersed himself in the political and cultural history of Bourbon France. The extravagant life led by the French court with its festivities, poetry, theatre, opera and music fascinated Ludwig II so much that he commissioned plays, concerts and operas to be performed in the French manner.

During this period, the Versailles project went under the codename of 'Meicost-Ettal', an anagram of the Sun King's famous pronouncement: 'l'état, c'est moi'. "It's supposed to be a sort of temple to fame in which I can honour the memory of King Louis XIV," was how Ludwig II put it.

The Bavarian monarch's 'second Versailles' is indeed a monument to the Bourbons, a prime symbol of the absolutist monarchy which was ultimately to elude his

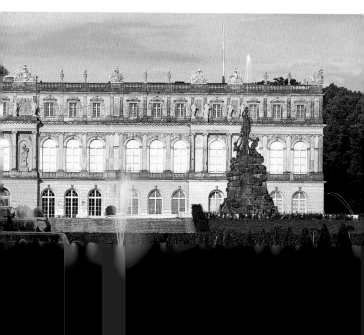

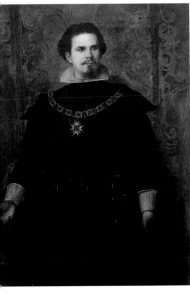

Franz von Lenbach, Portrait of Ludwig II as Grand Master of the Order of the Knights of St Hubertus, 1878/80, King Ludwig II Museum

grasp. Viewed in this light, Herrenchiemsee Palace is fictional architecture. As Ludwig II wrote to his friend Richard Wagner on 3 January 1872, he felt justified in remaining in his proper sphere so as "not to be dragged down into the mire of mundane things." Instead, he persisted in dwelling on "the poetic ideal of monarchical sublimity and solitude."

Bowing to public protest against felling ancient forests, Ludwig II decided in autumn 1873 to buy Herreninsel and resolved to build his new palace on it. After numerous aborted plans, a project worthy of Versailles was finally carried out under the supervision of the architect Georg von Dollmann. He had managed to survey the site by October 1873; on 1 February 1874 he was dispatched to Paris and Versailles to have another good look at the original. In August that same year Ludwig II finally made his pilgrimage to the colossal palace built by his idol, the Sun King.

From 18 April 1876 detailed plans existed for building and financing the palace. Dollmann's cost estimate totalled 7 million guilders to cover a period of sixteen years from 1878 to 1893. The estimated costs of plans made for the grounds handed in by Carl von Effner, Garden Architect to the Court, dated 14 April 1876, ran to 1,522,573 fl. The cornerstone of Herrenchiemsee Palace was laid on 21 May 1878. Construction work progressed, following the most recently approved plan of 31 October 1878 and, by spring 1879, work on the interior could begin. Ludwig II paid his first lengthy visit to Herreninsel from 29 September until 7 October 1881 to inspect the Great Hall of

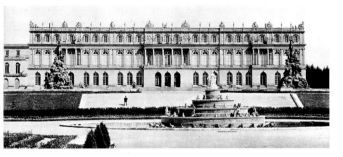

The palace, west façade, photo c. 1887, as it was a year after the king's death

Mirrors and the royal bedchamber in the Grand Apartments, which had been finished. The Court Architect Georg von Dollmann was rewarded for his achievement by being promoted to Chief Court Architect.

Work on the Lesser Apartments in the style of Louis XV continued to drag on while finishing touches were being added to the Louis XIV Grand Apartments. On 1 September 1884 the king discharged Dollmann because he was unable to guarantee that he could keep to the approved schedule. On 16 October Julius Hofmann was appointed as Dollman's successor. Hofmann managed to complete the sumptuously appointed, showy Lesser Apartments in 1884/85. Ludwig II had been staying from late September until early Octo-

By 1886 only three main wings of the much larger complex planned had been completed

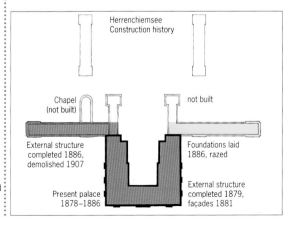

Herrenchiemsee Construction history

Chapel (not built)

not built

External structure completed 1886, demolished 1907

Foundations laid 1886, razed

Present palace 1878–1886

External structure completed 1879, façades 1881

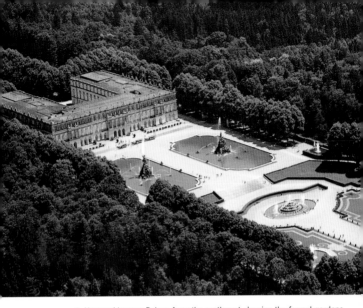

Herrenchiemsee Palace from the northwest showing the formal gardens and the densely wooded parkland on both sides

ber in Herrenchiemsee since 1881. By 1885 the king was able to occupy his new apartments. Then work slowed down, finally coming to a standstill for lack of funds. "It grieves the heart to see such well-organised workshops, manned by the most skilful of workmen who have been brought together over a period of many years, and to realize that all this, which has cost so much effort, shall no longer be maintained," wrote Hofmann bitterly on 23 September 1885.

Since the 'second Versailles' was so far from Munich on a remote island, construction work was fraught with difficulties. Keeping an army of labourers, skilled craftsmen and artists on such a scale functioning smoothly called for good leadership and efficient organisation. Georg von Dollmann, Franz Paul Stulberger and Julius Hofmann were the architects responsible both for construction and decoration. The painters Franz Widnmann, Eduard Schwoiser, Wilhelm Hauschild and Joseph Watter, the sculptor Philipp Perron, the court cabinet-maker Anton Pössenbacher, the tapestry and embroidery firm of Mathilde Jörres are only a few of the many artisans and businesses occupied in creating Herrenchiemsee. Their work was also instrumental in promoting the flowering of Late Historicism in Munich.

By the time Ludwig II, who had conscientiously supervised all plans and building, died in 1886, the Grand and Lesser Apartments, the Great Hall of Mirrors with the flanking halls and the showy state stairway at the south end had been finished. Of the lateral wings planned, the north tract was standing at this time, albeit only the shell. It was demolished in 1907.

Although the palace of the Sun King had been the model for Herrenchiemsee, the Bavarian island palace was not simply a copy of Versailles. It was, however, informed with the spirit of that age. In the sophisticated cultural context of the 19th century, an astonishing, indeed unique, work of art was created in full. Neo-Baroque and Neo-Rococo forms conformed with the canon developed for court art under Ludwig II. Recalling artists' studios and elegant salons, the atmosphere of the rooms, their colour schemes and lighting attest to the extreme sensitivity of perception cultivated at that time. Herrenchiemsee—a monument to ideal monarchy, reflected the dying embers of an enigmatic age.

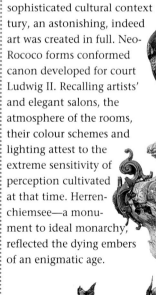

The monumental vase in the vestibule in the palace, with peacocks symbolizing Ludwig II's absolutist position

Entrance Hall and Vestibule

Neither the austere **Entrance Hall** (Room 1) nor the **Vestibule** (Room 2) on the ground floor give any hint of what is to follow. In the latter, however, a monumental vase sporting the monogram of Ludwig II and a vainglorious peacock evoke the rank of the builder: the peacock being a symbol of absolute monarchy.

The Grand South Stair

The Envoys' Stair in Versailles, although begun in 1671 and removed by 1750/52, was the model for the monumental Grand Stair (Room 3) which is sumptuously decorated and panelled in marble. Nonetheless, in Herrenchiemsee Palace, the imposing stairwell is unmistakably a creation of the late 19th century. Notably 'temple-like' in conception, it is lit evenly by a huge glass roof like the 'museum temples' of the period. The figure of Apollo, the Sun god ('Day') presides over the bright yet solemn light, accompanied by his sister, the Moon goddess Diana ('Night'). Cheerful murals, many of them scenes from Greco-Roman mythology, which—as the architect Dollmann observed—"represent the festive reception of the Prince as he enters," recall the processions and artists' festivities which seem to have given Ludwig II the vicarious pleasure he sought.

The Grand Apartments (*Paradezimmer*)

The Paradezimmer comprise a group of eight representative rooms of state (Rooms 4 to 11), decorated in the Louis XIV style and reminiscent of Versailles without, however, being exact copies. In the magnificence of their appearance and the sumptuousness of their appointments they might even be said to surpass Versailles in some respects. Thematically these rooms of state are linked with the Sun, signalizing the spirit of the age of Louis XIV.

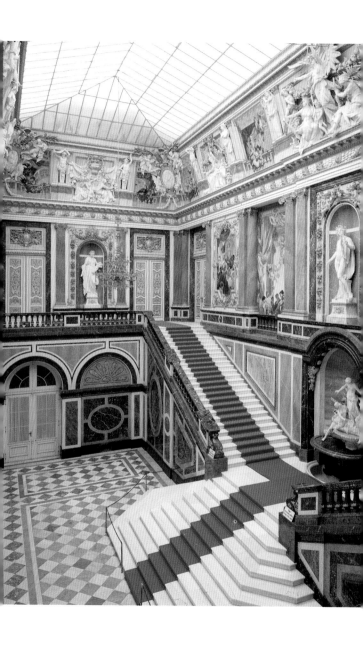

The Grand South Stair

The Halberdiers' Hall (*Hartschiersaal*) and the **First Antechamber**. A ceiling painting *The Triumph of Mars* (Franz Widnmann, 1882) summarizes the iconographic programme of the Halberdiers' Hall (Room 4), which bristles with such martial subject matter as the campaigns and battles fought by Louis XIV. The halberds set up here would have more appropriately symbolized the guard of honour at Versailles than the Bavarian monarch's bodyguards, whom he styled halberdiers. The mood lightens in the First Antechamber (Room 5), where the ceiling painting depicts Dionysus and Ceres entering the king's apartments in triumph (Wilhelm Hauschild, design 1879). The other paintings, scenes from French court life during the reign of Louis XIV, are also peaceful in tone. Begun in 1885, the overwhelming Neo-Rococo armoire was left unfinished.

The Second Antechamber. Nearly twice the size of its model in Versailles, the Second Antechamber (Room 6), is also known as the 'Bull's-Eye Hall'. This vast space was an original creation by Ludwig II. The enormous ceiling painting (Eduard Schwoiser, 1881) glorifies both Day and Night: Aurora, the goddess of the Dawn and of Light rises from the ocean in her triumphal chariot to dismiss her spouse, the Titan Astraeus, Lord of the Night and the Stars, with a morning kiss. The other paintings in the room also allude to the Sun King, who is represented by an equestrian statue (Philipp Perron, 1885).

The King's Bedchamber. As the setting for the 'lever du roi' and 'the coucher du roi', the first and last audience of the day granted by the French king, the royal bedchamber assumed the ceremonial function of a throne room at the court of Louis XIV. The King's Bedchamber at Herrenchiemsee (Room 7) was the result of a protracted aesthetic process in which Versailles figured only vaguely as the model for this masterpiece of unabashed formal opulence. Steeped in the sacred dignity

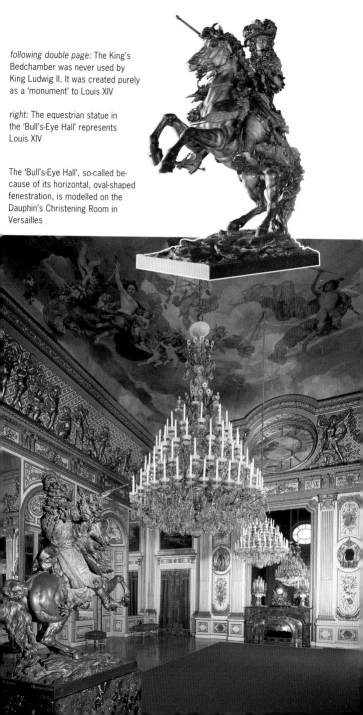

following double page: The King's Bedchamber was never used by King Ludwig II. It was created purely as a 'monument' to Louis XIV

right: The equestrian statue in the 'Bull's-Eye Hall' represents Louis XIV

The 'Bull's-Eye Hall', so-called because of its horizontal, oval-shaped fenestration, is modelled on the Dauphin's Christening Room in Versailles

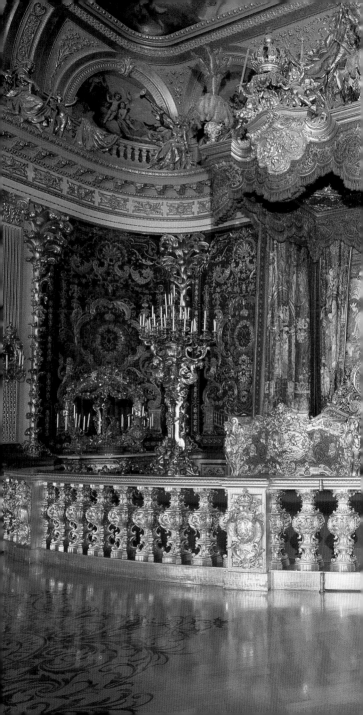

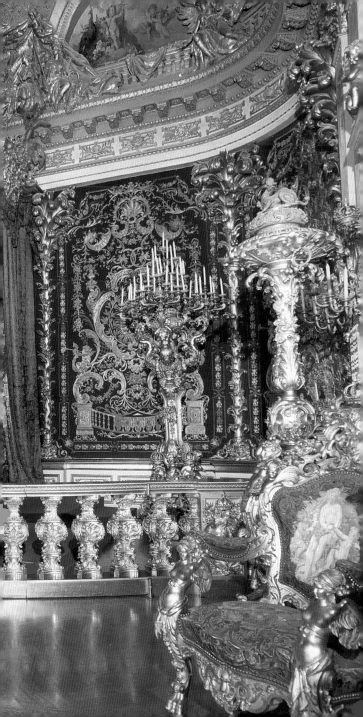

The Council
Hall

of majesty, it was a 'monument', not so much intended for use as for 'show', as Ludwig II himself put it.
Resplendent in gold, red and white and sporting a
magnificent polychrome bed with a gilt balustrade, the
room is crowned by an overwhelming ceiling painting featuring the pantheon of Mt Olympus (Eduard
Schwoiser, 1881). The dominant figure is Apollo in the

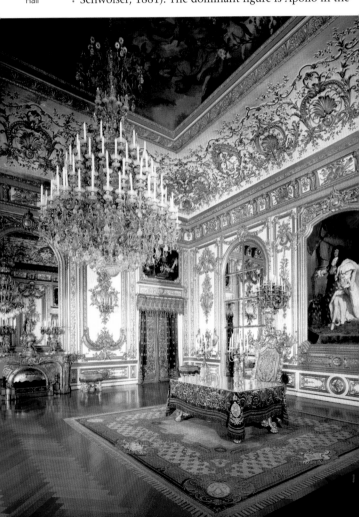

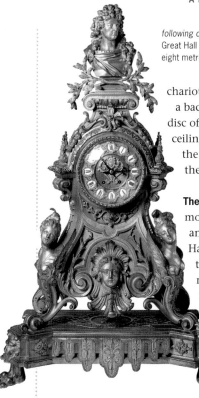

following double page: The 98-metre-long Great Hall of Mirrors at Herrenchiemsee is eight metres longer than that at Versailles

chariot of the Sun set against a backdrop of the fiery disc of Day suffusing the ceiling with a fan of rays: the very apotheosis of the Sun King.

The Council Hall. Decorated more austerely in gold and white, the Council Hall (Room 8) is more than the sum of such reticent details as the fine tissue of decoration below the cornice. The carpet on the floor, the desk, the ceiling and the

Council Hall, mantelpiece clock with bust of Louis XIV

king's chair are all overt references to the copy of the state portrait of Louis XIV (Jules Jury after Hyacinthe Rigaud) on the rear wall of the room. The Sun King is also evoked in the French manner by elegant clocks. The ceiling painting (Eduard Schwoiser, 1883) is appropriate: surrounded by the Council of the Gods, Jupiter is issuing orders from a lofty throne for Mercury to convey to mortals.

The Great Hall of Mirrors. Primed by the stage scenery he enjoyed at command performances in the Munich Court Theatre, Ludwig II commissioned a Great Hall of Mirrors for Herrenchiemsee (Room 9) as a copy of its namesake in Versailles. The furnishings missing in Versailles were to be reconstructed to recapture the 'original lustre' of the model. Since the Herrenchiem-

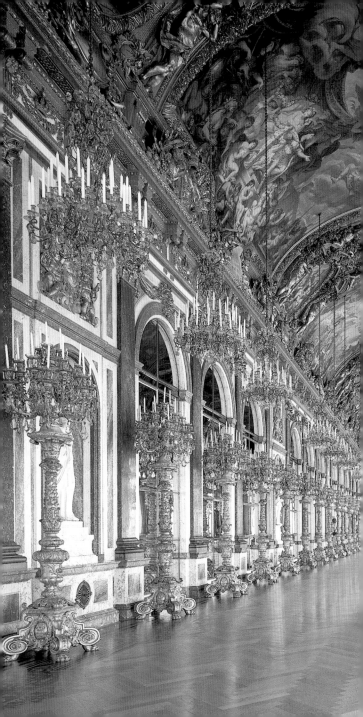

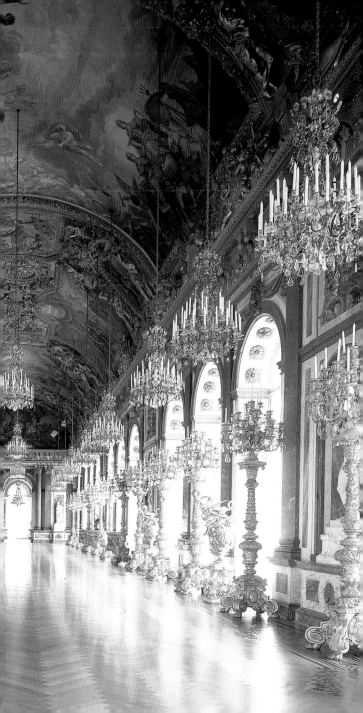

see room is eight metres longer, slightly wider and 70 cm higher than the original, the vaulted ceiling could be articulated with sculptural effects. Begun by several artists in 1880, the paintings in the Herrenchiemsee ceiling reserves follow the Charles Le Brun cycle in Versailles in reflecting French history through the Sun King's exploits. The room is replete with replicas of ancient sculpture in alcoves and the busts of Roman emperors as well as 33 chandeliers, 44 candelabra, ornamental vases and tubs for orange trees. Mirrored arcades reflect the westering light admitted by a high row of windows.

The Halls of War and Peace. Abutting the Great Hall of Mirrors at its north and south corners, these rooms, too, are copies of salons in Versailles. A copy of the allegorical oval portrait of the Sun King by François Lemoine hangs above the fireplace in the Hall of Peace (Room 10).

The lunettes and saucer domes of the Herrenchiemsee room are decorated with allegorical paintings on the theme of peace. A stucco equestrian relief of 'Louis XIV as a general of antiquity', a replica of a work of this type in Versailles by Antoine Coysevox, dominates the Hall of War (Room 11). The central ceiling painting shows Bellona, the Roman goddess of war, with a portrait of Louis XIV. The theme of war is treated throughout in the same vein.

The Lesser Apartments

Begun in 1992, this group of rooms (Rooms 13–19) in the north wing of the palace was reserved for King Ludwig II. Although vaguely modelled on the private apartments of Louis XV in Versailles, the Bavarian king's living quarters reveal an eclectic blend of influences, with borrowings from the Hôtels de Soubise and de Toulouse in Paris, Fontainebleau and even the palaces in Würzburg and Munich. The predominant style, however, is the court Neo-Rococo already established

right: As at Versailles, the Hall of Peace and the Hall of War (shown here) flank the Hall of Mirrors

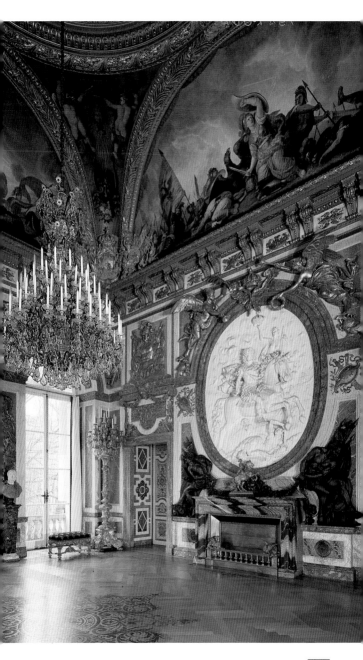

by Ludwig II at Linderhof and carried over to the design of his opulent state coaches. Blue, symbolizing night, is the key colour in the Lesser Apartments. The idea was to counterbalance the fiery red of the sun blazing in the Grand Apartments.

The King's Bedchamber and Cabinet. Decorated in white and gold, the King's Bedchamber (Room 13) is panelled in the French manner and lavishly decorated with carving. The alcove for the bed is separated from the rest of the room by a balustrade. Wall panels hung with blue watered silk form a subtle transition to the sumptuous blue silk velvet coverlet on the king's bed, which is richly embroidered in gold. A scene featuring 'Louis XV Conquering Vice' is embroidered in coloured silks on the rear wall. Figurative elements integrated in the overall decoration scheme include such pagan scenes as 'Apollo in the Chariot of the Sun' (on the ceiling above the baldachin), 'Venus Reclining' (between statues of 'Venus' and 'Adonis' (the footboard of the bed). A globe of blue glass rests on an ornate stand, the king's night-light. A dressing-table with a basin and ewer, a sumptuous hassock for prayers, a holy waterfont and a lapis lazuli console supporting a bust of Louis XV add stagy touches of eerily eclectic grandeur and solemnity. Off the bedroom there is a small cabinet (Room 14) appointed in the style favoured by Queen Marie Antoinette (not open to the public).

The Study and Blue Salon. The decoration of the King's Study (Room 15), all in gold on a white ground, culminates in mythological figures and scenes in relief in the bead moulding below the cornice and on the adjacent zone of the ceiling. The curtains add a touch of colour; so do the paintings. The north wall sports an inset copy of the state portrait of Louis XV (Jules Jury after Jan van Loo), which dominates the room. The overdoors continue the cycle narrating important events from the reign of Louis XV begun in the King's

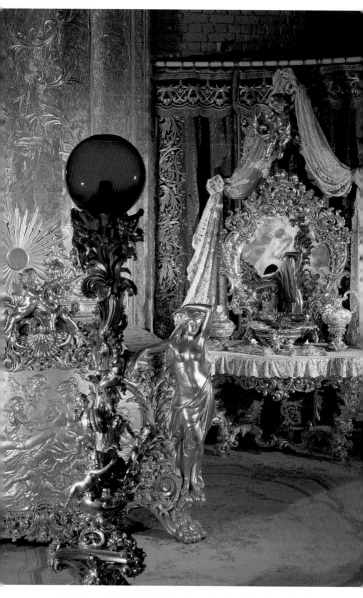

While the red of the King's Bedchamber refers to the Sun King, the blue in the King's Bedchamber in the Lesser Apartments aludes to Ludwig II as the king of the night

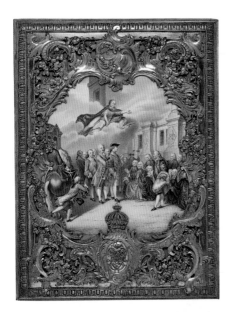

Writing-case with painting on porcelain, *Louis XV before the Hôtel de Ville in Paris*, King Ludwig II Museum

right:
The Study with the king's roll-top desk

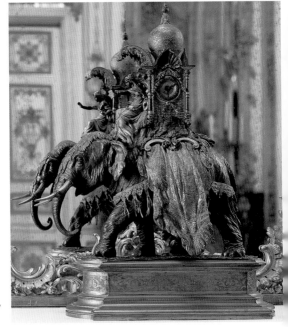

The 'Elephant Clock' in the study

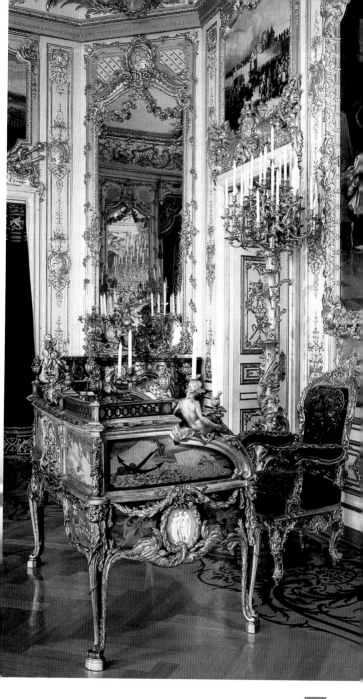

Bedchamber (Room 13). The roll-top desk, made for the 1882 Paris Exhibition, is an updated version of the 'Bureau du Roi Louis XV de France' in the Louvre. A scattering of elegant novelty clocks—an 'Elephant Clock', a 'chiming clock' and a 'Mountain Clock' (albeit now in Room 8)—relieves the overall effect of studied formality.

The Blue Salon (Room 16, not open to the public), a cabinet of mirrors, functioned as a sort of antechamber to the King's Study. It is also known as the 'Hunt Room' because it is decorated with hunting motifs. Mirrors give the fantastically opulent décor a surreal twist.

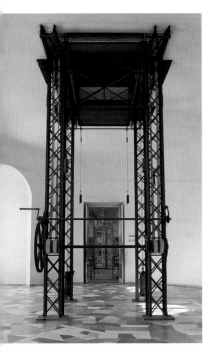

The mechanisim for lowering the dining room table into the room below so that the king wasnot disturbed during mealtimes by footmen

The Dining Room and Porcelain Cabinet. The oval dining room (Room 17), decorated in red, white and gold, is modelled on the Hôtel de Soubise in Paris. Scenes from the Cupid and Psyche myth fill the spandrels above the panelling. A huge Meissen porcelain chandelier hangs from the centre of the vaulted ceiling above the dining-table. The table stands on a section of the floor which can be lowered into the room below. This meant that the table could be set and raised into the dining room again without disturbing the king's privacy. As Theodor Hierneis, the king's personal chef, divulged, Ludwig II preferred to dine alone although dinner was often served for four as he used to imagine himself in the company of such eminent guests as Louis XV and Madame de Pompadour.

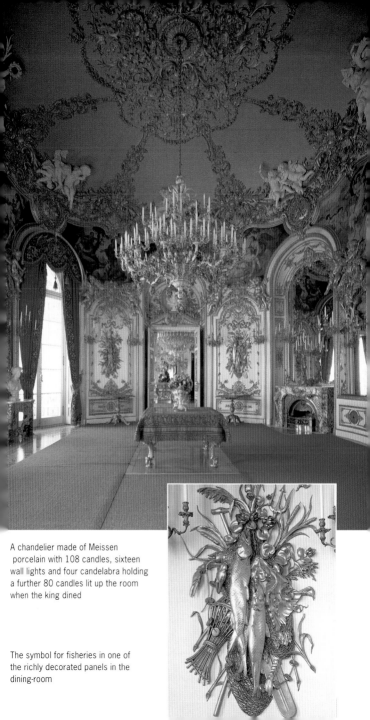

A chandelier made of Meissen porcelain with 108 candles, sixteen wall lights and four candelabra holding a further 80 candles lit up the room when the king dined

The symbol for fisheries in one of the richly decorated panels in the dining-room

The dining room could once be reached through the Porcelain Cabinet (Room 18, no direct access), which is also oval in plan so that the two rooms together form an aesthetic whole. Modelled on similar rooms in both Versailles and Fontaineblau, the Porcelain Cabinet is referred to as the 'Oval Salon'. The clear articulation of the room is echoed and enhanced by its reticently elegant décor. The surface of the walls creates the impression of porcelain. Despite the strength of the colours they appear as delicate and

The Porcelain Cabinet is the most intimate room in the palace

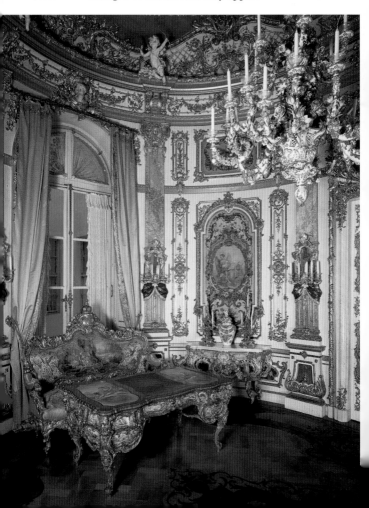

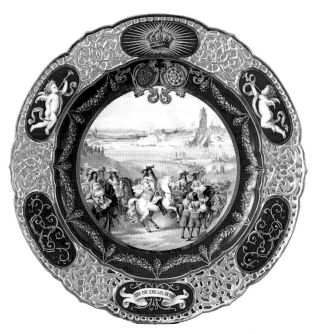

Dessert plate depicting Louis XIV entering Dunkirk in 1658,
King Ludwig II Museum

soft as pastel shades. The Meissen porcelain objects
which include chandeliers, mirror frames and con-
soles, vases, candlesticks and amoretti can be displayed
to their best advantage in these surroundings. The
doors are panelled with paintings on porcelain including a female allegory juxtaposed with a portrait of
Ludwig II. An exquisite suite of chairs is set off by a
handsome rosewood desk inlaid with painted porcelain. In keeping with the other rooms in the royal
apartments, the parquetry of the floor with intricate
intarsia is, in itself, a magnificent work of art.

The Little Hall of Mirrors. The king's private apartments
are preceded by the Little Hall of Mirrors (Room 19, no
direct access) with two corner salons. The length of
these rooms was determined by the Great North Stair
(Room 20, never completed). The Little Hall of Mirrors
is a more intimate, miniature version of the Great Hall
of Mirrors (Rooms 9, 10, 11). In its appointments and

furnishings it echoes the Grand Stair (Room 3) leading to the more spacious state rooms. It is modelled on similar rooms in St Cloud and the Hôtel de Toulouse in Paris.

The King's Bath and the Dressing Room. Via the unfinished North Stair (Room 20), the tour of the palace brings the visitor back to the ground floor. In the **Passage** (21), the workings of the lift mechanism for raising and lowering the dining table are explained. The royal Bath (Room 22) is a grand oval hall boasting a marble swimming-pool. A panoramic fresco depicts 'Venus in Vulcan's Forge', the 'Birth of Venus' and 'Venus at Her Toilet'. A circular stair winds up from the King's Bedchamber (Room 13) to the Dressing Room (Room 23), in which all the elements of a hall of mirrors have been brought together: gilt trunks of palm trees interlaced with branches and foliage weave lofty mirror-panelled walls into a surreal synthesis of labyrinthine Neo-Rococo and a Thousand and One Nights.

The North Stair

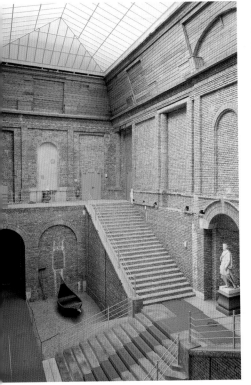

right:
The Little Hall of Mirrors

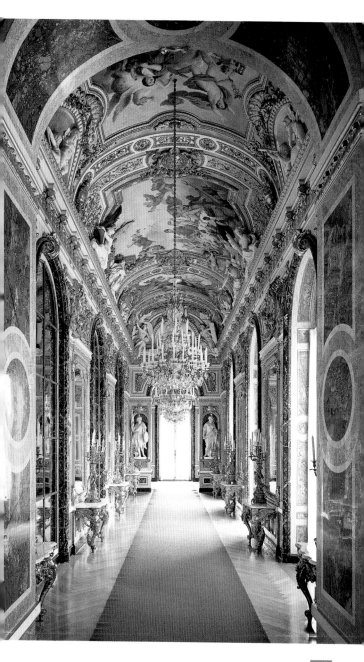

The idea of founding a King Ludwig II Museum dates back to the years immediately following World War I, when art historians began to study and inventory the art and architecture of Ludwig's reign. Inaugurated in 1926 in Herrenchiemsee Palace, the museum closed in 1962 for curatorial reasons.

In 1987 the King Ludwig II Museum was re-opened in the south wing of the palace. Twelve newly-styled rooms on the ground floor are filled with exhibits drawn from the decorative and fine arts of the period. The museum surveys Ludwig's tragic life story from birth to his untimely and mysterious death. Importantly, welcome light is shed on his real-life role as an innovative patron of the arts.

The first section is succinctly biographical. Symbolically representing Ludwig's birth (1845), ascension to the throne (1864) and death (1886) are his christening gown, his coronation regalia and his death-mask. Paintings and sculpture, prints and contemporary photographs illustrate his life story, linking it with Bavarian and European history.

Another thematic section deals with King Ludwig II as a patron of the arts. The 'King's palaces and castles' are represented by a telling selection of art objects. A room is devoted to the first bedroom from Linderhof. Although the royal apartments in the Munich Residence were destroyed in the war, their furnishings and appointments fill several rooms in the museum. The conservatory in the Residence, demolished after Ludwig II died, is also documented here.

Models represent projects which remained castles in the air, including a St Hubert Pavilion intended for Linderhof and Falkenstein Castle. A room is devoted to Ludwig's numberous projects incorporating Near and Far Eastern elements.

Selected exhibits show that work commissioned by Ludwig II bears comparison with any produced for more orthodox patrons of the arts in Vienna and Paris, which were the leading centres of design in his day. Inkstands for desks, basins and ewers for royal wash-

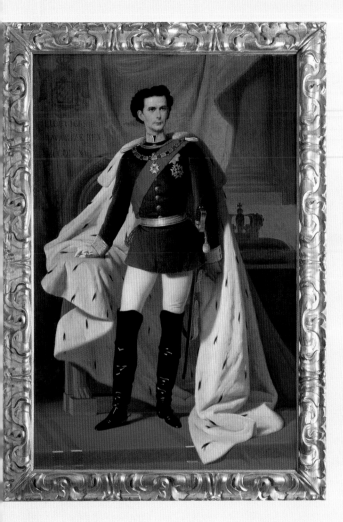

Ferdinand Piloty the Younger, Ludwig II in the uniform of a general and coronation vestments, 1865

stands and even an ormolu knife-box imaginatively made in the form of a ship are all distinctively designed and beautifully worked.

The king's role as a patron of music is shown by his support for Richard Wagner. The composer's fame is documented in the museum with portraits and personal possessions such as scores and contemporary cartoons.

A Tour of the Museum

Room 1: **Entrance**. Visitors are immediately confronted with the celebrated portrait of King Ludwig II in the uniform of a Bavarian general. Painted in 1865 by Ferdinand Piloty the Younger, the portrait shows the monarch at twenty as the handsome and dignified young man who was widely admired by his contemporaries. Formal photographss of Ludwig II, his brother Otto and their parents are displayed in an adjacent room.

Room 2: **Birth – Reign – Death**. The king's christening dress, coronation robes and death-mask are moving witnesses to his life and career. Busts of Ludwig and his brother Otto as children, made in 1855 by Johann Halbig, are particularly appealing.

Furniture from the former King's Apartments in the Munich Residence

Rooms 3 and 4: **The King's Apartments in the Munich Residence**. Some of the sumptuous furnishings saved from the Munich dining room, bedroom and audience chamber of King Ludwig II are exhibited here. The throne and baldachin are particularly fine.

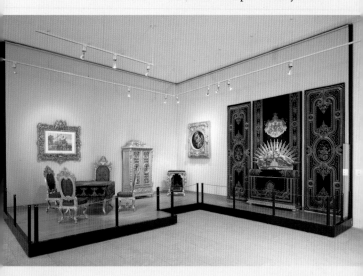

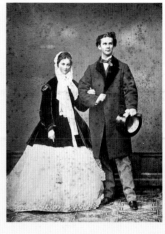

Notable objects include a basin, covered bowl, glasses and a ewer of blue glass mounted in metal made for the washstand in the king's bedroom. Display cases full of Bavarian coins, medallions, plaquettes and an array of decorations are intriguing. The monumental statue of Ludwig II executed in 1870 by Elisabeth Ney is regarded as the most arresting full-length portrait of the King.

Room 5: **Betrothal**. In 1867 Ludwig II was engaged to his cousin, Sophie Charlotte. The official engagement portrait, a pair of portrait vases and the robes of state intended for the wedding ceremony that never took place poignantly recall this engagement.

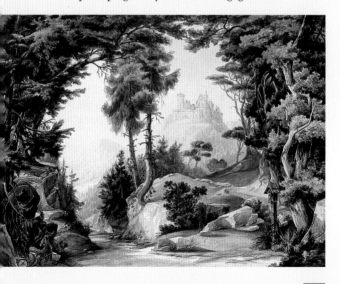

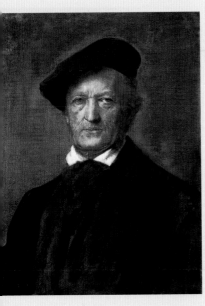

Franz von Lenbach, *Richard Wagner*, 1874

Room 6: **Ludwig II as Grand Master of the Order of the Knights of St George**. The magnificent desk from the king's study in the Residence is eye-catching. His inkstand and writing materials—an inkwell and pens, a dish, a folder, a paperweight, seal and writing-case—are prominently displayed. The regalia worn by the king as Grand Master of the Order of the Knights of St George are in a display case together with Lorenz Gedon's model of St George (1868). Gabriel Schachinger's monumental state portrait (1887) shows the king in full Baroque regalia as Grand Master.

Room 7: **King Ludwig II and Richard Wagner**. The exhibition in this room centres on a model of the Munich opera house designed by Gottfried Semper and a model for a second theatre he planned to build in the Munich Glass Palace. Numerous personal documents commemorate the friendship between King Ludwig II and Richard Wagner.

Room 8: **Neuschwanstein and Falkenstein**. Models for stage sets of Wagnerian operas lead thematically into Neuschwanstein and Falkenstein. Neuschwanstein is represented by a tiled stove. Falkenstein, a projected castellated fortress, never advanced beyond the original model, which is displayed here.

Room 9: **Linderhof and Herrenchiemsee**. Plans of the buildings and grounds at Linderhof and Herrenchiemsee are on display. A model for a garden statue and an ornamental vase for the landscaped park are from

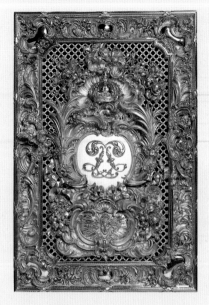

Writing-case with Ludwig II's monogram, probably Ferdinand Harrach, c. 1883

Linderhof; a model for the sculpture planned for the Apollo basin has come from Herrenchiemsee. Further, designs for art objects and pieces of opulent porcelain typify the appointments at Herrenchiemsee and Linderhof. The splendid knife-box in the shape of a ship come from Linderhof. Exhibits in this room also include a model for the St Hubertus pavilion, which was to be built nearby.

Gallery to Rooms 8 and 9. These display cases are filled with a selection of objets d'art, including a porcelain service with scenes from the life of Louis XIV, writing-cases, inkstands, wallets, cheroot-holders, spectacle-cases, ornamental receptacles, miniature bottles and china Easter Eggs.

Room 10: **The first royal bedchamber at Linderhof.** Finished in 1873, the furnishings were removed in 1884. However, many of the pieces and ornaments have been preserved. Plans for this opulent state bedchamber are also on display.

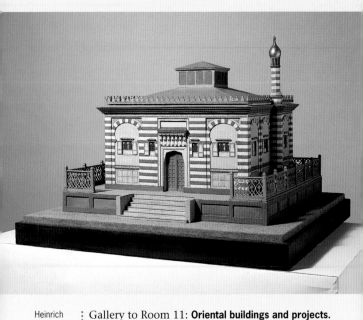

Heinrich Döll, Model for the Moroccan House at Linderhof

Gallery to Room 11: **Oriental buildings and projects.** Designs for a Wagnerian Hunding Hut near Linderhof and two drinking horns are a prelude to plans for buildings and projects with a distinctly oriental or Far Eastern flavour. Exhibits include the mountain hunting lodge at Schachen, the Moorish kiosk at Linderhof, a Moroccan house at Linderhof, a Chinese summer palace and a project for a Byzantine palace. Models, plans, drawings and art objects are on display.

Rooms 11 and 12: **The conservatory in the Munich Residence**. Enlargements of photographs and an oil painting of the conservatory, which was finished in 1871, commemorate what was a superb example of its kind. A canoe from the small pond within the conservatory itself is also on display. The glass roof and samples of exotic flora convey some idea of what it was like. A marble bust of King Ludwig II by Elisabeth Ney (1869/70) marks the end of the tour of the museum.

While on his second trip to Paris in 1874, King Ludwig II fulfilled the dream of a lifetime by spending two days and a night in Versailles. There he celebrated his 29th birthday and his name-day. He was particularly intrigued by the fountains in the park, which were turned on specially in his honour. The visit to Versailles proved fruitful for his plans for the gardens at Herrenchiemsee. Although the terrain around Linderhof was not suitable for extensive land-scaping since the Graswang Valley is particularly narrow, the island on Chiemsee provided sufficient space for gardens on a scale rivalled only by those at Versailles.

Plans drawn up by Carl von Effner, the landscape architect to the court, specified a park stretching from the lake in the east to the water in the west. In its opposing axis, the park extended almost as far as the north and south shores of the island. The grounds were to be laid out on a vast scale, incorporating almost half the area of the island.

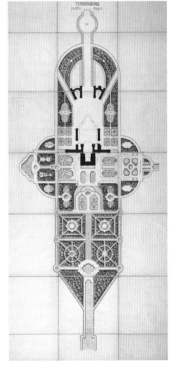

On 14 April 1876 Effner submitted his final plans for approval with an estimate of the cost of 'laying out a large garden like Versailles on Herren-wörth.' Based on geometric patterns

Carl von Effner, Plan of the gardens at Herren-chiemsee, 1876

49

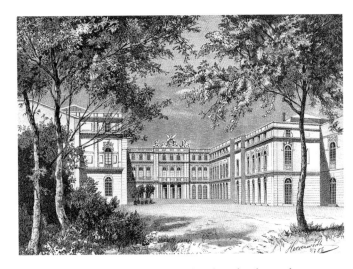

The Marble Court, woodblock print made from a drawing dated 3 July 1886

in the French manner, the plans for the gardens borrowed freely from Versailles: in the west the main axis comprised a sequence of water terrace, steps, the Latona Fountain, flower beds, lawn, the Apollo Pool and a canal. The shrubberies to the north and south of the wings of the main building also evoked Versailles. The approach to the Palace began in the east with

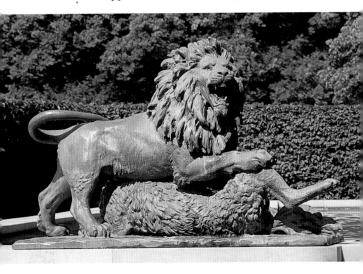

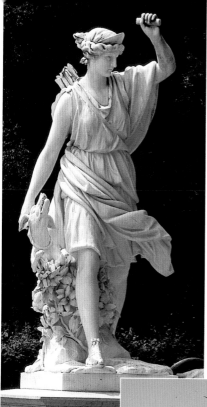

a jetty for the king's boat. Via a broad 'avenue' in the grand English manner, visitors arrived at the forecourt with its two coach house wings. From there visitors reached the Great Court and finally the central Marble Court.

Although rivalling Versailles in scale, the park at Herrenchiemsee is not a copy of it. Distinctively eclectic, it is a 19th-century garden in the Historicist

Diana, north-west marble fountain, by Johann N. Hartmann, 1885/86

right: The Fama Fountain in the northern basin on the water terrace

left: One of a group of hunters and their quarry around the marble fountain on the upper parterre

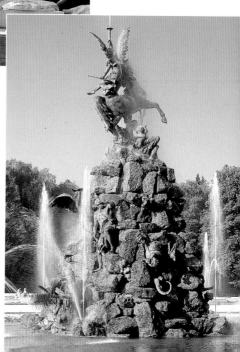

manner. The sunbursts and thrusting axial systems which so aggressively dominate the landscape at Versailles are all but imperceptible here. The Bavarian park is subtly distinct from the rolling hills, forests and meadows of its wider surroundings without losing the impact made by geometric designs contrasting with the natural landscape.

The gardens at Herrenchiemsee were never finished as originally projected. At the time they were being planned priority was given to levelling the terrain. It was 1882 before laying out the gardens began. The canal to the lake was dug in 1884.

right: Mythological figures in lead, modelled on those at Versailles, skirt the basin on the upper parterre

Carl von Effner originally intended the geometrically laid out gardens along the west front to be broader than those seen today. The canal down the central axis flows directly into the lake

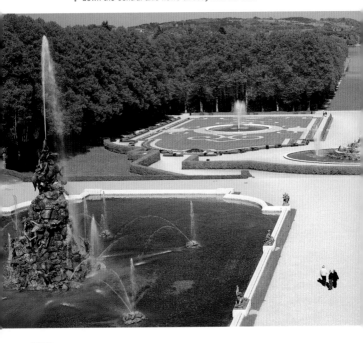

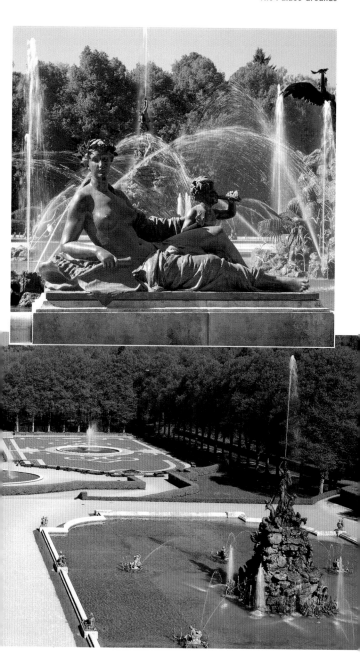

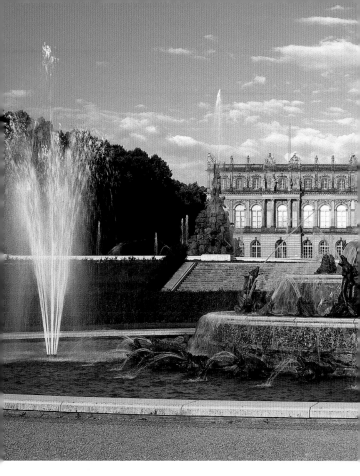

The Latona, Fama and Fortuna fountains form a focal point in front of the palace and provide a truly royal performance

By the time King Ludwig II died on 13 June 1886 the gardens forming the main axis had been largely completed and the fountains were in operation. Effner's successor as the landscape architect to the court, Jakob Möhl, supervised the laying out of the grounds from 1884 onwards. The scaled down design which can be admired today reflects the gardens much as they were when they were originally planted in 1888.

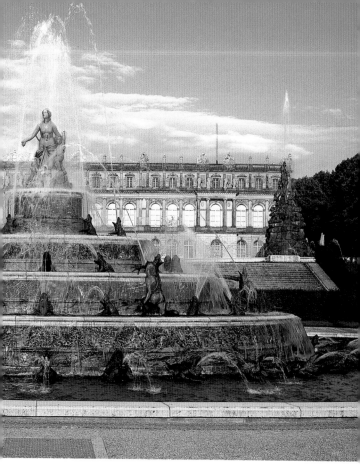

The Approach and the Marble Court. The avenue leading up to the palace was originally planned to link the jetty on the eastern shore of the island with the Marble Court in the grand manner of the time. Today's more modest design follows a plan drawn up in 1888 which included two tree-lined avenues bordering a narrow strip of lawn terminating at the Marble Court. Paved with black and white marble, the formal court is surrounded by the three wings of the Palace. The façades are in the style of Louis XIV. A clock adorned with a sculpture of Fama (Fame) and other allegorical figures crowns the architrave of the central tract.

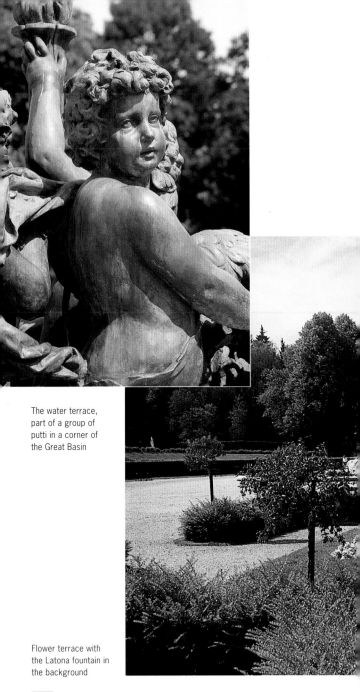

The water terrace,
part of a group of
putti in a corner of
the Great Basin

Flower terrace with
the Latona fountain in
the background

The Water Terrace. The upper terrace or water terrace fronts the west façade, which is clearly modelled on Versailles. The fountains (in full working order again since 1994) are also positioned at spots corresponding to those occupied by fountains at Versailles. Two **marble fountains** stand at the corners of the terrace: at the north-west corner is a fountain with a sculpture depicting hunters and the hunted and statues of the goddesses **Diana** and **Venus**; at the south-west corner its counterpart boasts statues of **Flora** and **Amphitrite** (Johann N. Hautmann, 1885/86).

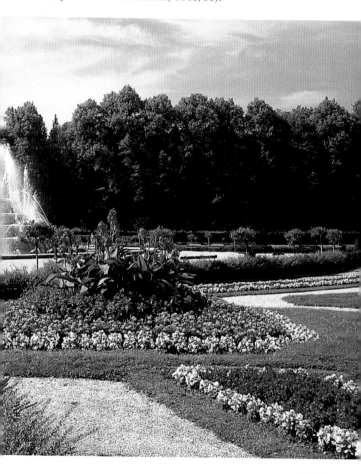

Although the statues grouped round the edge of the water are copies of sculpture at Versailles, refreshingly original touches enliven the fountain basins at Herrenchiemsee. To the north the **Fama Fountain** dominates the scene. A massive pyramidal rock forms the base 'of a group of statues that includes a horse, celebrating the theme of fame. Fama, a winged allegorical personification, triumphs over Envy, Falsehood and Hatred (Rudolf Maison, 1884/85). In the water, six smaller rocks spouting water jets are clustered around this focal point. The **Fortuna Fountain** to the south is centred on the goddess Fortuna on the Wheel of Fortune (Wilhelm von Rümann, 1884/85). Six putti astride dolphins encircle the goddess of fortune. With their plumes of rising and falling water, fans of spray, turbulent cascades and glittering veils of crystal drops, the Herrenchiemsee fountains are subtly integrated in the overall design. Against the dark mid-summer foliage of limes, they join the **Latona Fountain** on the flower parterre in providing an aquatic spectacle unrivalled for variety and splendour.

The Flower Terrace. Steps lead down to the lower parterre or flower terrace planted with two ornamental flower borders. Two round basins with fountains form a focal point. A borrowing from Versailles, the **Latona Fountain** at the steps is a sparkling prelude to the fountains in front of the palace (Johann N. Hautmann, 1883; restored in 1970/72). Versailles is again evoked in the fountain with its two jets and three basins arising from an ellipsoid pool and crowned by marble statues of the Titaness Latona accompanied by her children Apollo and Diana. In a satisfyingly startling departure from Ovid's Heroides, Latona is depicted here being refused water by Lycian peasants, whom she punishes by changing them into frogs.

The Apollo Pool and Grand Canal. A long strip of lawn ('tapis vert'), fringed with paths, trees, and hedges, leads down from the flower terrace to the Apollo Pool.

As in Versailles, a fountain surmounted by a sculpture of 'Apollo Driving the Chariot of the Sun' was planned but never carried out. The Grand Canal, an artificial body of water which was dredged again in 1993, is a well-known motif at Versailles. Here it forms the last section of a long ribbon of gardens, opening a vista to the lake to disclose a restful panorama of hills on the western horizon.

The palace and grounds built for Ludwig II are fully integrated in the cultural landscape of Herreninsel in Lake Chiemsee, a spot so remote that it was almost inaccessible in his day. This most romantic of monarchs created the perfect fusion of Alpine vistas to the south, gently rolling hills to the west, ancient forests and quiet shores with water meadows, a tapestry of gardens and the picturesque remains of monastic buildings.

With the Alps as a backdrop, the island location presents a beautifully romantic setting

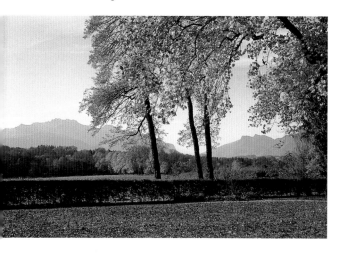

Other guide books in this series include:
Neuschwanstein (ISBN 3-7913-2368-7)
Linderhof (ISBN 3-7913-2369-5)
Nymphenburg (ISBN 3-7913-2370-9)

Front cover: The garden front of the palace
Back cover: (*top left*) Ferdinand Piloty, Ludwig II in a general's uniform
and coronation vestments, 1865 (see p. 43); (*top right*) mantlepiece
clock with bust of Louis XIV (see p. 27); (*bottom*) the Great Hall of Mirrors
(see pp. 28/29)

Photographic credits: all pictures are from the archives held at the
Bavarian Administration of State Castles, Palaces, Gardens, and Lakes
(incl. photos by Lucinde Weiß, Maria Custodis, Tanja Mayr and Rainer
Herrmann), with the exception of pp. 14/15, 19, 28/29, 34 (bottom),
37 (bottom), 51 (bottom), 54/55: Achim Bunz, Munich; p. 50: Klaus Plage-
mann, Prien; pp. 8, 9 (top), 10, 51 (top), 56, 57, 59: Elmar D. Schmid,
Gauting; p. 6: Kerstin von Zabuesnig, Starnberg

Plans of palace and grounds: Nordmann + Nordmann, Munich

Cartography: Anneli Nau, München

© content and layout:
Prestel Verlag, Munich · London · New York, 2001

Prestel's 'Museum Guide *Compact*' series, covering Bavaria's castles,
palaces, gardens and lakes, is published in cooperation with the Bavarian
Authority of State Castles and Palaces, edited by Peter O. Krückmann

Die Deutsche Bibliothek – CIP Einheitsaufnahme data is available
ISBN 3-7913-2378-4

Prestel Verlag
Mandlstrasse 26, 80802 Munich, Germany
Tel. (089) 38 17 09-0, fax (089) 38 17 09-35;
4 Bloomsbury Place, London WC1A 2QA
Tel. (020) 7323 5004, fax (020) 7636 8004;
175 Fifth Avenue, New York, NY 10010
Tel. (212) 995-2720, fax (212) 995-2733

Translated from the German by Joan Clough-Laub, Munich
Edited by Christopher Wynne
Designed and typeset by Norbert Dinkel, Munich
Lithography by ReproLine, Munich
Printed by Peradruck, Gräfelfing
Bound by Attenberger, Munich

Printed in Germany on acid-free paper
ISBN 3-7913-2378-4 (English edition)
ISBN 3-7913-2375-X (German edition)